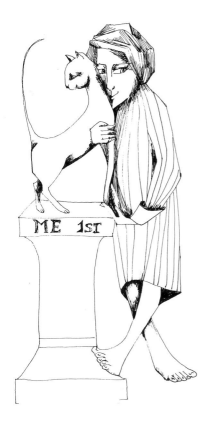

Cooking for Cats

Cats are more than capable

of cooking for themselves

so try to have some culinary

magic on your shelves

and caterers for cats take care to

always make a beeline

for recipes that might appeal to

the domestic feline.

D1465726

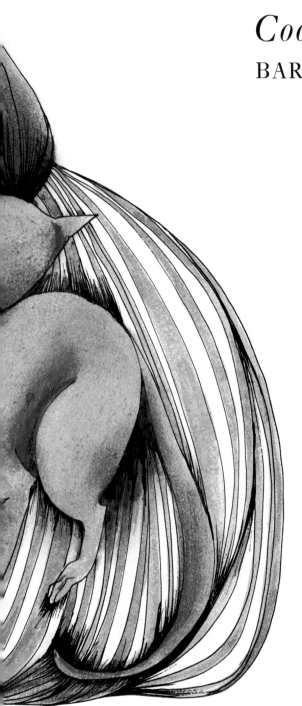

Cooking for Cats

BARRY CASTLE

Methuen · London

First published in 1985
by Methuen Children's Books Ltd,
11 New Fetter Lane, London EC4P 4EE
Text and illustrations
copyright © 1985 by Barry Castle
Printed in the Netherlands
by Deltaprint Holland

British Library Cataloguing in Publication Data

Castle, Barry
  Cooking for cats.
  I. Title
  823".914[J]   PZ7

  ISBN 0-416-52000-6

Barry Castle's original works of art
are exhibited exclusively
by Portal Gallery Ltd, London, England

Cooking for Cats

Noah's Cataclysm

Noah's sons were all engaged in loading up the Ark,
and in something of a flurry for the sky was getting dark.

They rounded up the animals and hurried them below,
the barometer was falling, it was coming on to blow,
and thankfully they battened down the holds when all were stowed.
They had had a lot of bother finding such a varied load,
for orders were there must be two of every form of life
for the purposes of breeding, a husband and a wife.

It stormed and rained for forty days, the Ark was splashed and pounded,
until a noise beneath the keel told them that they had grounded.

The first to step ashore
and put his foot on Ararat
was Noah's old companion,
the ginger galley cat.
And when they took the hatches off
the holds, and looked within
one hold was full of cats compressed
like sardines in a tin.

Though two of every species
were put aboard the Ark,
glib cats had cozened half the other
beasts to disembark.

Noah's vindication to
Jehovah was succinct:
'It's due to Cats the mastodon
and dodo are extinct,
the sabre-toothed tigers
and the roc and dinosaurs
were cruelly abandoned.'
But cats don't feel remorse,
they've got something special and
other beasts can't rival it,
built into their nature is a
powerful cat survival kit,
as long ago as Noah they were
busily contriving
that when every other race is done.
cats will still be thriving.

Big cats like big fish to eat

Since big cats like big fish to eat
a mermaid is a special treat.

It may be
– if you're not too hurried –
that you might like your mermaid curried
or, if that's too commonplace
why not a monster bouillabaisse?

First take all the inside out
and tightly stuff the vacant space
with twenty mice or thereabout,
(but save the ova in a jar
and label *Mermaid Caviar*).
Now put the mermaid down to stew
with slugs and snails and one or two
ingredients that I've forgotten –
ah yes,
a bouquet garni tied with cotton.

As they wash their paws and faces
tell your cats to say two Graces
for as this mermaid is Siamese twins
they're getting twice the vitamins.

Mock mockingbird

St Francis said, 'I have a yen to be a vegetarian,
eating meat's a beastly vice so you cats leave off eating mice.
You hear the tune this bird is humming?
It comes through his internal plumbing,
when *he* indulged himself with meat his singing wasn't half as sweet.'
His pets resentment was acute: 'But hummingbirds exist on fruit!
Cats don't live on cantaloupe, can't we have mock turtle soup?'

The saint relented, pity stirred, 'I'll make a meatless mockingbird
of cornflour mixed with heather honey, put nut cutlets in its tummy,
cover it with cream of rice and leave it for a while on ice.'

He gave the tail a final tweak and put a cherry in its beak.
'While it's cooling over there I'll offer up a little prayer:
      Hear me Saviour; heretofore
      these cats were classed as carnivore,
      please add a little extra flavour
      to this mockmockingbird cadaver?'

As they lifted fork and knife the bird was briefly brought to life
and from the freezer thin and sweet its voice sings 'Grace before we Eat'.

The Mockingbird was carved and eaten:
'It's good enough for Mrs Beeton!'
the cats said, and sincerely paid this culinary accolade.
They soon left off tormenting mice and dying went to Paradise
where, fitted out with wings and lyre, they were accepted for the choir.

Gentle Francis wept with pride to see his cats beatified.

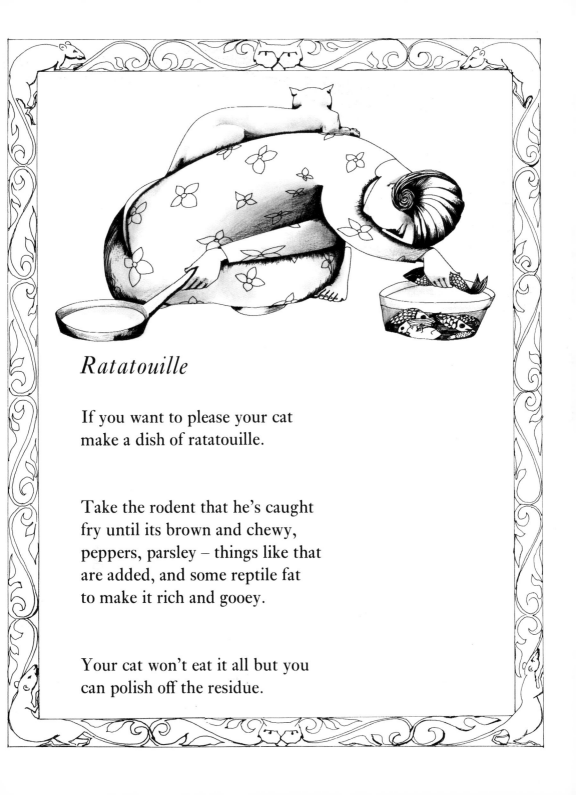

Ratatouille

If you want to please your cat
make a dish of ratatouille.

Take the rodent that he's caught
fry until its brown and chewy,
peppers, parsley – things like that
are added, and some reptile fat
to make it rich and gooey.

Your cat won't eat it all but you
can polish off the residue.

Once I had a cat called Mouse

She had the courage of a rabbit
and an aggravating habit
of sidling round the skirtingboard.
I coaxed, caressed, *implored* in vain
to make her be a cat again,
I smacked her till my fingers smarted
'Try to be less chicken-hearted.'
Mouse had little sense of fun
for when I said 'cat got your tongue?'
she went back in her hole and made
an impregnable barricade.
Finally, despite the price,
I got professional advice.
'What palliative have I missed?'
I asked the cat psychiatrist.
'She's not demented – here's my fee –
You should try homeopathy.' *
What a brainwave! In a trice
I'd made some spicy sugared mice.
Mouse ate them all and licked her lips
and then – a cat apocalypse!
She bit the man who brings the post –
(I must have under? over-dosed?)
She chased an Afghan up a tree –
defiled the pavement horribly –
was guilty of such villainy
(too infamous to catalogue)
I had to change her name to Dog.

*This method treats the ill in situ with a hair of the dog that bit you.

Cats concert

I know a tawny owl who has

a penchant for progressive jazz,

and all the cats would like a chance

to ask the clever owl to dance,

For every cat is simply itching

to dance the owl into the kitchen,

and on a toasted crumpet set

the trumpet playing owlet.

They anticipate – whereas

the owl continues playing jazz.

Soul food

There's a saying 'cats feel blue
without another cat to woo'.
I'm inclined to feel more yellow
when I haven't got a fellow.

To all cats that aren't mated
this recipe is dedicated.

> Take a kilogram of cod,
> preferably caught in Britain,
> with a sharp knife carve into
> the shape of a seductive kitten.
> Coat it well in muffin batter,
> bake – and with triumphant clatter
> call your cat with drum and trumpet
> for what you have is catfish crumpet.

Cheers!

This cat has a chronic thirst.

     'I'll have a gin-and-tonic first
          then scotch-and soda, pink chartreuse . . .'

     He'll swallow any type of booze,
every day he's getting thinner
since he drinks not eats his dinner.

     'Call a cat an alcoholic?
          spirits make my spirits *rollick*.'

But he's paler, more Byronic,
daily weaker, wan, laconic.

     'Hangovers? Sure I got 'em,
          my mouth tastes like a parrot's bottom

I'll make him a restoring dose
of dog's hair mixed with Worcester sauce
for now he's pleading

     'Be a brick . . .
        Please . . .
           Give a catatonic . . . .'

Smoked hamster

Pam and Kate are keen on liberating
anything that comes within their sights,
they've gone to endless trouble to ensure that
every pet's conversant with his rights e.g.,
the Right that every cat has got
to have a hamster in his pot.

Their carrot-coloured cat's called Stealth.
He has told his womenfolk
(despite the danger to their health),
to cure *his* hamster
in the best Havana smoke.

A Cat in Eden

In Eden lived a man called Adam and Evie who was Adam's madam.
There wasn't much to do and they eventually tired of play
so, starting with a plea for pardon, they asked the Great Ones of the Garden
'. . . we're awfully happy here, and yet . . . are we allowed to keep a pet?'
From somewhere a commanding voice directed them to take their choice,
a cat? a dog? performing fleas? but Adam wanted none of these,
'I'm pretty sure my heart will break if I can't have the garter snake.
 I'll call him Spot. Do believe me, soon you'll come to love him, Evie.'

The Snake was keeper of the Tree of Knowledge. The monotony
of living coiled around the trunk had made him something of a drunk
so Adam was a perfect godsend, boon companion – drinking friend.
But just above where Adam sat there was an artful jealous cat.

'Psst! How about some apple tart?' he hissed at Eve, who in her heart
(concealed within her birthday suit), longed to eat forbidden fruit.
Eve's mouth watered covetously, 'Cook,' said Cat, 'this fruit for me?'

A version of what happened next is in the King James' standard text –
the snake is blamed, but we know that the proper culprit was the cat.

A sweet tooth

This is Claud
who has a notion
nothing good
comes from the ocean:
'Fish at best are wishy-washy
outside scaly, inside squashy.
The Creator's plan was faulty
making all those oceans salty.
He should instead have made
                   them sweet
and full of yummy things to eat.'
If Claud could have a thousand
                   wishes
he'd fill the seas with chocolate
                   fishes.

A Christmas Treat

Christmas Day is incomplete
without a festive dish to eat.
Surprise your cat with Roast Dalmatian
it makes a tasty combination
meat and stuffing *and* plumduff.

Though this year he's had enough
your feline chum will be agog
for *next* year's Roast Plumpudding Dog.

(Who so distrusts the atmosphere
his heart is in his mouth all year,
he's got a strong suspicion
              that
                Santa Claus
              was
                  a
                    CAT!)

Killing with kindness

My cat Chrysanthymum's
memory lingers –
he died of a surfeit of goldfish fingers.

When Lionel cleared his goldfish pond
Chrysanthymum got overfond
of goldfish fillets fried and stewed
and baked in cream and barbecued.
A dish of goldfish soused in sherry
twice a day was customary.
If I'd been wiser there's no doubt
he wouldn't have developed gout.

I buried him in yonder hummock
when the gout went to his stomach
and put a tombstone at his head
        'This message is for cooks,' it said.
        'Save yourself lifelong regret:
        DO NOT overfeed your pet.'